Looking at . . . Baryonyx

A Dinosaur from the CRETACEOUS Period

THE NEW
DINOSAUR
COLLECTION

For a free color catalog describing Gareth Stevens' list of high-quality books, call 1-800-542-2595 (USA) or 1-800-461-9120 (Canada). Gareth Stevens' Fax: (414) 225-0377.

Library of Congress Cataloging-in-Publication Data

Green, Tamara, 1945-
 Looking at— Baryonyx / written by Tamara Green ; illustrated by Tony Gibbons.
  p. cm. — (The New dinosaur collection)
 Includes index.
 ISBN 0-8368-1274-3
 1. Baryonyx—Juvenile literature. [1. Baryonyx. 2. Dinosaurs.] I. Gibbons, Tony, Ill.
 II. Title. III. Title: Baryonyx. IV. Series.
QE862.S3G74 1995
567.9'7—dc20   94-36822

This North American edition first published in 1995 by
Gareth Stevens Publishing
1555 North RiverCenter Drive, Suite 201
Milwaukee, Wisconsin 53212 USA

This U.S. edition © 1995 by Gareth Stevens, Inc. Created with original © 1994 by
Quartz Editorial Services, Premier House, 112 Station Road, Edgware HA8 7AQ U.K.

Consultant: Dr. David Norman, Director of the Sedgwick Museum of Geology,
University of Cambridge, England.

Additional artwork by Clare Herronneau.

Printed in the United States of America

2 3 4 5 6 7 8 9 99 98 97 96 95

Looking at . . . Baryonyx
A Dinosaur from the CRETACEOUS Period

by Tamara Green

Illustrated by Tony Gibbons

THE NEW
DINOSAUR
COLLECTION

Gareth Stevens Publishing
MILWAUKEE

Contents

5   Introducing **Baryonyx**

6   Super-claw

8   **Baryonyx**'s bones

10   The story of fossils

12   **Baryonyx** discovered

14   In **Baryonyx**'s time

16   Greedy beast

18   If dinosaurs had survived . . .

20   Dinosaur data

22   The clawed gang

24   Glossary and Index

Introducing
Baryonyx

What a very curious-looking creature **Baryonyx** (BAH-REE-<u>ON</u>-ICKS) must have been, with its awesome jaws and those enormous, lethal claws on its front limbs!

One stab with these body weapons, and the poor victim would not have stood much of a chance.

Just look how sharp they were!

The bones of **Baryonyx** were dug up for the first time only a few years ago, in 1983. Before then, scientists did not know it had even existed.

So what do scientists know about **Baryonyx** now?

When and where did it live? What did it eat? And why was it given this odd-sounding name? Who first found its remains? How was a picture formed of this terrifying beast?

There's a lot to find out about **Baryonyx** and the prehistoric world it inhabited. Let's get started . . .

Super-claw

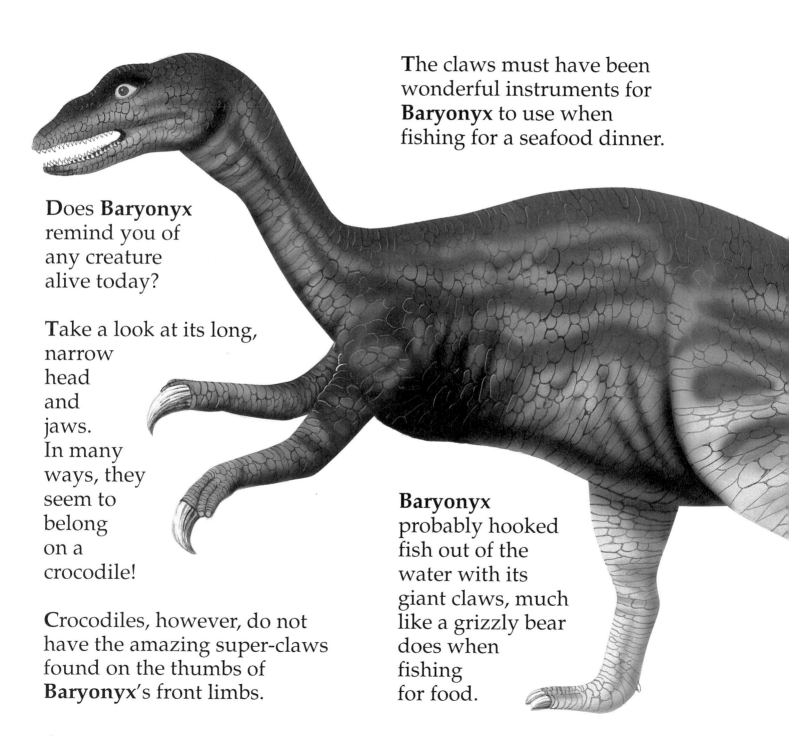

The claws must have been wonderful instruments for **Baryonyx** to use when fishing for a seafood dinner.

Does Baryonyx remind you of any creature alive today?

Take a look at its long, narrow head and jaws. In many ways, they seem to belong on a crocodile!

Crocodiles, however, do not have the amazing super-claws found on the thumbs of **Baryonyx**'s front limbs.

Baryonyx probably hooked fish out of the water with its giant claws, much like a grizzly bear does when fishing for food.

Scientists know for sure that **Baryonyx** ate fish because they have found fossilized fish scales in the dinosaur's remains.

But **Baryonyx** may also have been a predatory carnivore, killing smaller dinosaurs when it wanted meat. At times, it may have scavenged, too, feeding on creatures that were already dead.

At 30 feet (9 meters) in length, **Baryonyx** was as long as a bus. It was heavy, too, and weighed about 2 tons – that's as heavy as about 25 average-sized men.

Danger lurked for fish whenever **Baryonyx** was on the prowl!

Imagine coming face-to-face with such a monster. It's just as well no humans existed when dinosaurs roamed Earth. In fact, modern humans did not evolve until many millions of years after dinosaurs became extinct.

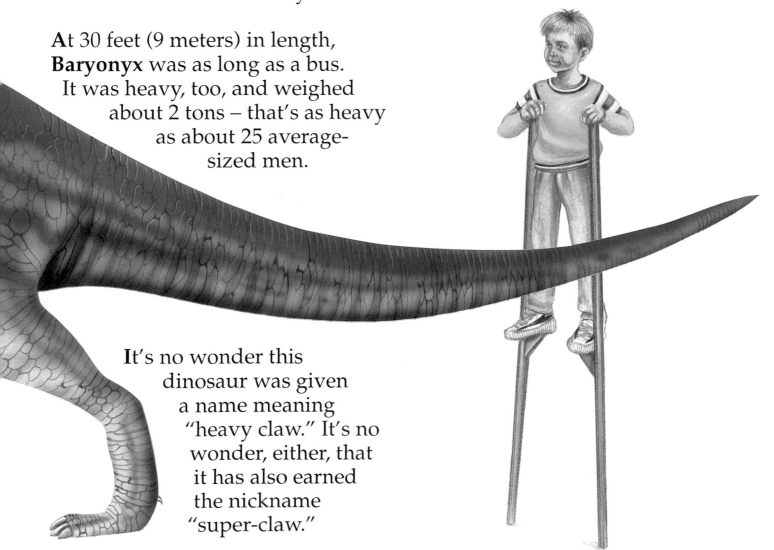

It's no wonder this dinosaur was given a name meaning "heavy claw." It's no wonder, either, that it has also earned the nickname "super-claw."

Baryonyx's bones

Strangely, **Baryonyx** had about twice as many teeth as most other meat-eaters.

From the skeleton that experts have pieced together, we can see that **Baryonyx** had an elongated skull supported by a long neck.

If you study its head, you will also see that **Baryonyx** had a small bump, or crest, on top of its snout.

Its back legs were sturdy. The front limbs were quite powerful, too. Some scientists think **Baryonyx** might have been able to move around on all fours, like a quadruped (four-legged creature).

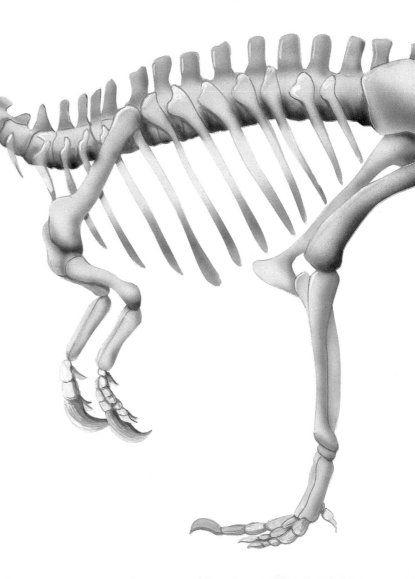

These teeth were ideally designed for grasping at slithery, wriggling victims — whether fish or land creatures. The teeth were largest at the front and smaller toward the back of **Baryonyx**'s mouth.

Paleontologists first found **Baryonyx**'s remains next to the bones of an **Iguanodon** (IG-WA-NO-DON) — another dinosaur with a weapon on its thumb. This suggests that the two creatures may possibly have died fighting.

Now take a look at **Baryonyx**'s tail. It was almost as long as the rest of its body and tapered toward the tip.

Scientists think that **Baryonyx**, when alive, may have weighed a couple of tons, or even more. This leads the scientists to believe the dinosaur's great claws were not on its back feet, like those of **Deinonychus** (DIE-NO-NIKE-US).

Baryonyx would have been too heavy to stand on one hind leg and slash with the claw on its other hind leg, like **Deinonychus** did. **Baryonyx**'s front limbs, however, were certainly strong enough to carry such claws.

Just imagine how excited paleontologists must have been when they were first presented with **Baryonyx**'s huge claws and the bones from its enormous skeleton!

The story of fossils

Paleontologists dig up and study fossils — the remains of animals, such as dinosaurs, or plants that lived millions of years ago. But how exactly are fossils formed in the ground?

Let's take **Baryonyx**'s remains as an example. It died many millions of years ago — perhaps of old age. Or maybe it was killed in combat.

Either way, its skeleton would gradually have become covered with sand and mud after its flesh had decomposed or been eaten by scavengers.

Over millions of years, layers and layers of mud and sand would have built up over **Baryonyx**'s skeleton. The lower layer would have slowly turned into rock.

Minerals and chemicals then filled small holes in **Baryonyx**'s bones, making them solid. This is a process known as fossilization.

Slowly, too, Earth's layers of rock moved a little. Over even more millions of years, the fossilized bones of **Baryonyx** were then forced upward, causing the whole skeleton to break up. Eventually, a claw came through to the surface and was discovered by humans.

Sometimes, however, bones and teeth may decompose completely.

All that remains is a hole in the rock, which paleontologists call a *mold*.

Various substances can gather inside a mold after it has formed. These substances then form a fossil that is made from different materials from the original, but which has the same shape. If this occurs, the fossil is known as a *cast*.

Another form of fossil is known as a *trace fossil*. This can be the fossil of a dinosaur's footprints or even its droppings.

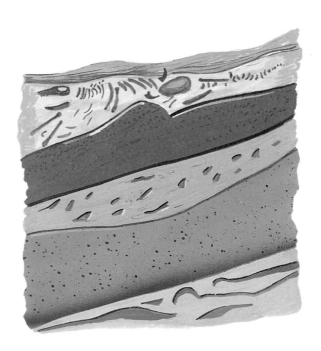

Baryonyx discovered

New types of dinosaurs are being discovered all the time. Not long ago, in 1983, an amateur fossil collector, Bill Walker, was out in a clay pit near Dorking in Surrey, England, looking for fossils.

Suddenly, he came across a strange claw that was sticking out of the mud. No one had ever seen anything quite like it. The enormous claw measured 12 inches (31 centimeters) along its outside curve. What sort of creature could have had a claw like that?

Walker asked the experts, but no one could identify it. Scientists from the Natural History Museum of London, led by the paleontologist Alan Charig, were so curious that they sent along a team to look for more fossils in that clay pit.

Here, they found many more bones scattered around a small area. Fortunately, a bulldozer had not yet crushed them. All the bones seemed to belong to the same creature. The scientists managed to reconstruct almost all of a huge dinosaur.

Finding so many pieces of a skeleton instead of just fragments was cause to celebrate. Scientists found the bones to be about 124 million years old. This was the best skeleton of a flesh-eating dinosaur ever found in England.

Scientists also thought this dinosaur must have looked a little like **Allosaurus** (AL-OH-SAW-RUS). But this creature was quite unusual because of its narrow snout, which was about 3 feet (1 m) long. It also had fairly long front limbs.

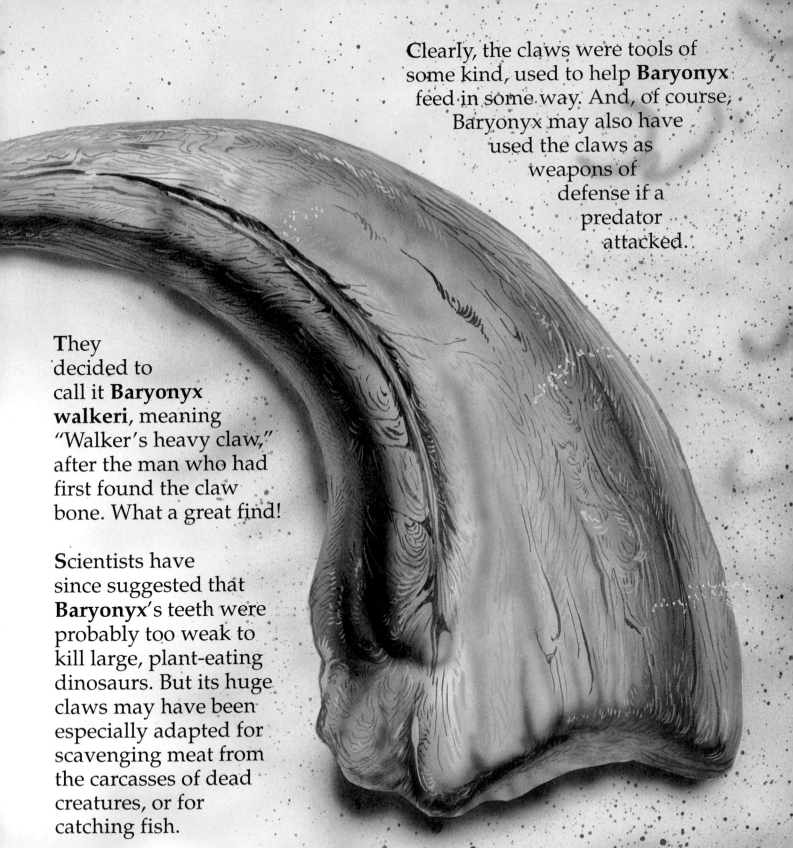

Clearly, the claws were tools of some kind, used to help **Baryonyx** feed in some way. And, of course, Baryonyx may also have used the claws as weapons of defense if a predator attacked.

They decided to call it **Baryonyx walkeri**, meaning "Walker's heavy claw," after the man who had first found the claw bone. What a great find!

Scientists have since suggested that **Baryonyx**'s teeth were probably too weak to kill large, plant-eating dinosaurs. But its huge claws may have been especially adapted for scavenging meat from the carcasses of dead creatures, or for catching fish.

In Baryonyx's time

Imagine a scene about 120 million years ago in the area of the world we now know as England. These were Early Cretaceous times, and Europe and Africa were still joined.

14

Earth certainly looked different then. Seasons were just beginning to divide into spring, summer, autumn, and winter. Flowering plants, too, were a new sight on our planet.

Baryonyx spent its day fishing for food. There were many rivers and lakes at the time surrounded by rich vegetation. The climate was warm and wet. But **Baryonyx** also ate meat, and many smaller dinosaurs became its victims.

Other dinosaurs, such as **Iguanodon**, **Hypsilophodon** (<u>HIP</u>-SEE-<u>LOAF</u>-OH-DON), long-necked **Astrodon** (<u>ASS</u>-TROW-DON), and horny-beaked **Camptosaurus** (<u>CAMP</u>-TOE-<u>SAW</u>-RUS) roamed then, too. All had to beware in case **Megalosaurus** (<u>MEG</u>-UH-<u>LOW</u>-<u>SAW</u>-RUS) — the massive carnivore — threatened. Look out!

15

Greedy beast

The sun was just rising, and early morning light glistened on the water. The riverbank was slowly coming to life. Frogs darted here and there, disturbing lizards that were resting before the new day began. Fish were visible, stirring

Baryonyx was skilled at fishing and would find it easy to land a large one for breakfast. **Lepidotes** (LEP-EE-<u>DOE</u>-TEEZ), for instance, was about 3 feet (1 m) long and would provide a welcome feast.

under the surface. A hungry **Baryonyx** thought about how appetizing the fish would be. It had not eaten for several hours.

Baryonyx crouched by the bank, listening and watching for any movement in the water, waiting for the right moment to pounce.

This was it! **Baryonyx** stuck out one of its huge claws trying to grab **Lepidotes** as it approached. The fish, however, moved swiftly and was only scratched by the claw.

Baryonyx would not give up. It wanted that fish. Quick as a flash, the dinosaur entered the water, pursuing **Lepidotes** as rapidly as

Crouching beside the riverbank, **Baryonyx** was still enjoying its breakfast fish when it stopped and caught a whiff of **Iguanodon** in the air.

The young **Iguanodon** was only a few feet away. It might just do for lunch! Baby **Iguanodon** meat was bound to be tender and delicious.

it could. Poor **Lepidotes** now shivered in fright. **Baryonyx** stabbed again with its claw and then, quick as a flash, snapped up the poor victim in its jaws.

If dinosaurs

Let's have some fun imagining what dinosaurs might have been like today if they had not suddenly become extinct about 65 million years ago.

Of course, no one knows for certain how they might have evolved; we can only guess. They might have changed color over time, for instance. And the most intelligent dinosaurs with the biggest brains, like **Troodon** (<u>TROE-O-DON</u>), might have begun to walk upright, just as we do. In the fantasy picture shown here, **Troodon** looks like a clever creature. It might even have become clever enough to use a laptop computer.

18

had survived . . .

Some small dinosaurs — such as **Microvenator** (MY-CROW-<u>VEN</u>-UH-TOR) — might have developed the ability to climb. They could then have roamed the treetops, if they had not died out.

Protoceratops (PRO-TOE-<u>SER</u>-A-TOPS) — a plant-eater from Mongolia — might have become so tame that you could keep it as a pet and even ride on its back. That would have been an unusual way to get to school!

How do you think **Baryonyx** might have ended up? And what about such frightening creatures as **Tyrannosaurus rex**? Would human beings have been able to survive with such a terrible predator around?

Dinosaur dat

When **Baryonyx** was finally dug up from the clay pit where its thumb claw had first been discovered, almost three-quarters of its entire skeleton was found. Scientists, therefore, have a good picture of what this dinosaur looked like.

Powerful thumb claws

The remarkable claw on each of **Baryonyx**'s thumbs was about the length of your entire arm. What a terrifying threat to any smaller creature these thumb claws must have been! And what superb tools for fishing.

Crocodile jaws

Baryonyx's other outstanding feature was its crocodilelike head. You can see it above. Note the position of its eyes. And what an ugly bump it had on its snout! Its teeth were shaped like cones and had only slightly serrated edges — like those on a blunt steak knife — to help with slicing up its prey. But there were lots of them.

Sturdy limbs

Baryonyx's back legs were strong enough to bear all of its weight. But it could also walk using its hands and feet, if it chose. It would probably have gone on all fours when prowling near a river, watching for fish.

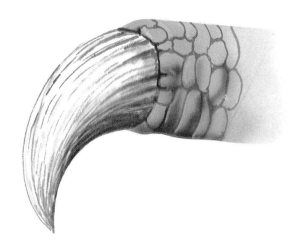

20

Feared predator

As well as enjoying fish, some scientists believe **Baryonyx** may have eaten meat at times, chasing after meals of small dinosaurs such as **Hypsilophodon**, a plant-eater.

Habitat

Remains show that **Baryonyx** lived in Early Cretaceous times in what is now England and may also have roamed other parts of Europe. Similar bones that have been found suggest it

Baryonyx had claws on its toes, but the two giant claws for which it is famous were on its front limbs.

Fish-eater

When scientists examined **Baryonyx**'s skeleton, they found scales and teeth from a fish known as **Lepidotes** in its rib cage. This indicated that **Baryonyx** had been a fish-eater.

may have lived in West Africa, too. Remember that much of the world was still one big landmass when **Baryonyx** wandered planet Earth. Remains of **Baryonyx** may be found elsewhere, too.

The clawed gang

No wonder **Baryonyx (1)** is often called "super-claw." Those weapons at the end of its thumbs were truly frightening.

But **Baryonyx** was not the only dinosaur to have useful claws.

Long-necked, peaceful, plant-eating **Diplodocus** (DIP-LOD-OH-KUS) **(2)**, from Jurassic North America, had a special claw on the inner sides of its front feet for stabbing predators.

1

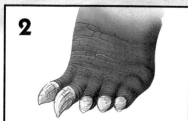

2

22

Deinonychus (3) had a large, curved claw on the second toe of each foot. When it needed to slash with this claw, it probably balanced on one foot, swinging the other leg so the claw could be put into action. Its enemy must have squealed in dreadful agony as this weapon struck its body and cut open its flesh!

The remains of **Noasaurus** (NOE-A-SAW-RUS) (4) were found in Argentina. It was a fierce predator, but it was only about 8 feet (2.4 m) long. Each foot had a powerful sickle claw powered by a strong muscle it used for attack.

Oviraptor (OH-VI-RAP-TOR) (5) was an even smaller dinosaur. Its strong, three-fingered hands had large claws, and it used these for grasping things — possibly the eggs it is known to have stolen from other dinosaurs and then eaten. (That's how it got its name, meaning "egg thief.")

3

4

5

GLOSSARY

carcass — the dead body of an animal.

carnivores — meat-eating animals.

evolve — to change shape or develop gradually over a long period of time.

extinction — the dying out of all members of a plant or animal species.

fossils — traces or remains of plants and animals found in rock.

predators — animals that capture and kill other animals for food.

prey — animals that are killed for food by other animals.

remains — a skeleton, bones, or a dead body.

scavengers — animals that eat the leftovers or carcasses of other animals.

snout — protruding nose and jaws.

INDEX

Allosaurus 12
Astrodon 15

Baryonyx: back legs of 8, 20; crested snout of 8, 12, 20; eating habits of 6, 7, 15, 16-17, 20, 21; front limbs of 5, 6, 8, 9, 12, 21; head and jaws of 5, 6, 8, 17, 20; physical characteristics of 7, 9, 20-21; as predatory carnivore 7, 8, 21; remains of 5, 7, 9, 10, 21; as scavenger 7, 13; skeleton of 8, 9, 10, 11, 12, 20, 21; super-claws of 5, 6-7, 9, 12, 13, 17, 20, 21, 22; tail of 9; teeth of 8, 9, 13, 20
Baryonyx walkeri 13

Camptosaurus 15
carnivores 7, 15
Charig, Alan 12
Cretaceous Period 14, 21

Deinonychus 9, 23
Diplodocus 22

evolution 18
extinction 7, 18

fossilization 7, 10-11, 12

Hypsilophodon 15, 21

Iguanodon 9, 15, 17

Lepidotes 16, 17, 21

Megalosaurus 15
Microvenator 19

Noasaurus 23

Oviraptor 23

paleontologists 9, 10, 11, 12
predators 7, 13, 19, 21, 22, 23
prey 20
Protoceratops 19

quadrupeds 8

Troodon 18
Tyrannosaurus rex 19

Walker, Bill 12, 13